How to Start, Run, and Grow a Bail Bond Business

An Essential Start-Up Guide with Practical, Real-World Advice from a Pro!

By

A. J. Turner

Copyright © 2020 – **Streets of Dream Press**

All Rights Reserved.

No part of this publication may be reproduced, stored in a retrieval system or transmitted in any form or by any means, electronic, mechanical, photocopying, recording or otherwise without the proper written consent of the copyright holder, except brief quotations used in a review.

Published by:

Streets of Dream Press

Cover & Interior designed

By

Renee Leadsman

First Edition

Contents

Introduction – My Experience 7

All About Bail Bonds 16

What is a Bail Bond? 23

    History of Bail Bonds 24

    Market Statistics 28

    Challenges in the Industry 31

How Do Bail Bonds Work? 34

How Do Bail Bondsmen Make Money? 38

    Ways to Make Money 40

    Typical Salaries 42

Characteristics of Bail Bondsmen 44

    A Good Reputation 45

    Patience 45

    24/7 Availability 46

    Detail Oriented 46

    Good Listener 47

    Good Interpersonal Skills 48

    Financial Backing 48

- Good Knowledge of Crimes 49
- Having Experience 50
- Why Should You Start a Bail Bonds Business? 51
  - A Needed Service 51
  - A Flexible Schedule 53
  - Daily Variety 54
  - Lucrative Entrepreneurship 55
  - Job Security 56
- Types of Bail 58
  - Citation Release 59
  - Recognizance Release 60
  - Cash Bail 60
  - Immigration Bail Bond 61
  - Property Bond 62
  - Surety Bond 63
  - Federal Bail Bonds 64
  - Transfer Bonds 65
- Starting the Business 66
  - Information First 66
  - Partner with a Well-known Surety Company 69

- Acquire State Licensing 70
- Jail Lists and Registration 71
- Pay Initial Fees 72
- Fulfill Legal Requirements 74

Legal Processes Concerning Bail Bondsmen 83
- Forfeiture 84
- Defense of Forfeiture 84
- Authority of Arrest 85
- Remission 85
- Rates of Premium 86
- Banned Locations 87
- Banned Activities 88
- Advertisements Regulations 89

Blunders to Avoid 91
- Suffering Many Forfeitures 92
- Failure to Recuperate Losses 94
- Failures in Marketing 95
- Failure to Face Challenges 97

Growing Your Business 100
- Stand Out 103

    Choose Helpful Software 103

    Marketing 105

Customer Service Skills 119

    Expertise in Bonding 120

    Ability to Patiently Explain Things to Clients 120

    Empathetic 121

    Have a Positive Attitude 121

    Offer Fast Service 122

Dealing With Bail Bond Jumpers 123

    All About Bounty Hunters 124

    Thinking Like a Bail Jumper 137

    Consequences of Jumping Bail 138

Conclusion 143

Introduction – My Experience

In the year 2001, my family and I were forced to pay $1,000 to bail my brother in law out of jail.

I was very disappointed at the time, but I had no idea that that would later open my mind to the promising opportunity in the bail bonds business.

Before then, I thought that one had to pay about 10% of the bail as a deposit, and then the bondsman takes another amount as the fee.

However, I later came to learn that the bondsman actually keeps the 10%. This got me thinking that it would be an outstanding business opportunity to build up some revenue for myself. I did extensive research on the business and decided to get into the industry.

My introduction to the business began while I was in college. I was lucky enough to land a job running bonds for fifty to eighty dollars a pop to a courthouse in New Jersey. When I finally graduated, I worked with a bail bondsman who became my mentor and taught me a lot of things to do with the business. After a few years and with the blessing of my mentor, I set out to start my own bail bonds business. It was not easy at first, but when I look back at the journey, I understand that it was worth the struggle.

I began the business at the age of thirty-two and ran it as a sole proprietor for years. After a few years in practice, my business grew and I gained two employees. I did not actually meet most of my clients before bailing them out of jail. This is because they were mostly behind bars. Normally, I would deal with other relatives, usually moms, girlfriends, and wives.

I would always charge a fee according to the rates customary to the state law. That is, the first $3,000 would attract a fee of about 10% of the amount, $7,000 would amount to 8% of the amount, and whatever amount above that would get 6%. For a defendant to work with me, whoever is bailing them out had to be able to pay the percentage of the fee required by the company.

Things would get very complicated at times. Sometimes I would come across defendants who would decide to jet off to another state. In such cases, I would be forced to recompense the court the full remaining amount that would be thousands of dollars.

With experience, I learned ways to minimize the risk. I began asking for collateral. Sometimes this collateral would be in the form of cash that would be an extra few thousand on top of the set bond. I would keep this amount safe in an escrow account. Another kind of surety would be a contract to the deed of a property or a car.

I also realized that it is very crucial to demand that one or two individuals with occupations and consistent income sign a pledge and settle on covering any extra losses that I may make. The collateral was dependent on the risk. If the risk was big, so too would the collateral be.

After about three years, I began bailing out 200 individuals per year. Intuition and skill in selecting those clients are two very important things you should have as a bail bondsman.

Sometimes, I would be forced to turn away prospective clienteles if I would sense that the defendant would probably jump bail or if I think that the family will not manage to cover his charges in case the defendant goes missing. I encountered a few defaulters but on very rare occasions.

For cautionary purposes, I would also write agreements on bail that would require that the defendant come to sign in at my office once a week. This was helpful because if a defendant fails to show up for a while, I identify a budding problem, and I begin working on it before they jump bail.

Sometimes, though rarely, the defendant would disappear. In this case, I would go to civil court and make an attempt at getting the cash from the family. This is a very tiresome and costly process that I always tried to avoid.

I have heard that some bail bondsmen would use bounty hunters when facing such a situation. However, when faced with such difficulty, I would seek the services of a licensed private investigator who would track down the bail-jumper. This is the case with most bail bondsmen.

Many of them prefer private investigators over bounty hunters. Many a time, members of the bail jumper's family would help me find the defendant. There is nothing as motivating in this business as losing money. It is very motivating for me and the individual backing up the bond.

My days of chasing down felonious perpetrators are now in the past. My business has grown over time, and as a man living with my wife and kids, chasing defendants has become something that I delegate to my zealous mentees.

It is the best thing in the world to grow in business and get to mentor other people who would continue with this business for years to come.

My office had to have ample security with barriers to some places. For instance, I would keep all the cash I handled in another interior room that would always remain locked. Only I and another trusted member of the company would be allowed access.

I did not have tight security because I was paranoid; it is because security is really crucial in this business. You never know who you are dealing with. You never know if a defendant is innocent or guilty, and if you are not cautious, you may get in real trouble and lose a lot of money.

Most of the people you may come across in the business are less privileged and from different disadvantaged backgrounds. It is, therefore, important that you practice caution at all times.

Many a time, the defendants I would deal with would be people charged with robbery of things like phones, laptops, other technological items, or even selling drugs. However, over time, the narcotics cases became fewer as identity theft, and credit-card frauds became more.

For this reason, intuition is a really good characteristic that a bail bondsman should have.

A lot of people kick-start their journey in the industry through working for a reputable company like I did.

You can eventually start and grow your own business.

Having your own business is preferable since you become independent and flexible.

Decisions like the kind of customers to help, when to work, the sort of bonds to agree on, as well as all other particulars pertaining to your services, are all yours to make.

You also get the satisfaction of having and growing your own business.

A bail bond business is a service that will always be on-demand, unlike some businesses that sway with the waves of the economy.

There will always be people committing crimes every single day.

Also, when people are unemployed or the economy is bad, there may be an increase in crimes like robbery or credit card fraud.

This business will never lack a source of income, as long as there is crime.

With time, you can always add to your pay, depending on the number of folks you help.

You also get to make more connections in the field as you progress with your career.

Depending on your experience and the state in which you work, your salary could vary significantly.

Nonetheless, you could hypothetically make an annual pay of about $50,000 to $80,000. Some go-to companies in some states even make $100,000 or more a year.

To own or be in control of a bail bond business, you must be registered as a bail bond agent and have an operations license.

Since the statutes in several states have a limit on who may get a bail bond agent license, the people below may not be given a permit to be employed at a bail bond business or even own a bail bond agency.

- Any person who has been convicted or pleaded guilty or no contest to a felony or a crime involving moral turpitude

- People working in any jail or jailers

- Employees in any sheriff's department, deputy sheriffs, and sheriffs

- Law enforcement agency employees or the police

- Attorneys

- People with the power to arrest or those with authority over prisoners

- Employees of a clerk in any court, people employed in a court, as well as judges

All About Bail Bonds

In the U.S, the number of people jailed in the past 15 years has grown tremendously. This trend has steadily grown upward since the 1980s. Still, the number of persons convicted of offenses has also remained the same in the preceding 15 years. What is really going on?

It is alarming to realize that more men and women remain in prison just because they cannot manage to raise the money for their bail. Most of these individuals have been charged for crimes that are mostly nonviolent.

The amounts for bail for these charges range from $500 to $750, mostly less than $1,000. This has seen many people like The Bail Project's Robin Steinberg, hold discussions about ending the injustice of bail. This is because when a person is incapable of affording and paying the bail money, he or she is forced to remain imprisoned until the date of their court hearing.

According to the 2017 Federal Reserve report, four in ten Americans could not afford to raise the $400 expense that is usually unplanned. This imprisonment is known as "pretrial detention" in the criminal justice system. It can last weeks, months, or in worst cases, years.

According to the United States Constitution, an individual is regarded as innocent until the time that they are proven guilty. This, therefore, means that there could be about 450,000 honest characters that are in jail at the moment. All this because they are too poor to afford bail.

The original intention of bail was never to form a system of justice that is two-tiered, i.e., one for the wealthy and another for everyone else. However, what we see and what many people experience is exactly in contrast to the intended purpose of the bail system.

For example, say you get arrested for a crime like being drunk and disorderly. The judge sets your bail at $15,000. This is the money that you are required to pay for you to be released before the date of your court hearing. If you present yourself at court when you are supposed to, you get the money back. If you fail to show up, you forfeit it.

Most defendants are not usually able to randomly come up with fifteen thousand dollars. Since most cannot afford that amount yet do not want to remain in jail any longer, most seek the help of a bail bondsman.

Now, this is where the business of bail bonds comes in. This business is growing more prevalent due to the fruitful returns that its investors gain. Investors in the industry stand a higher probability of acquiring more cash. This is despite the fact that the entire concept of investing in bail bonds involves high risk.

No matter the case, each investor in the bail bond business carries out an in-depth investigation to guarantee that the accused or his family entirely owns the asset held as security. For this reason, every investor must know and work with the lawyers of the accused. He or she should also seek to comprehend the details of the case prior to agreeing to invest in any bond.

It is also vital that an investor assures that the estate used for collateral is not under any mortgage. As an investor, you will customarily demand that the stake is not below 150%. For instance, if an individual is giving you an estate that does not show any growth, an appraisal ought to be carried out to ensure that its cost is higher than the value of the bond. Ordinarily, though the risks in the business are significant, the returns got on bail bonds are high.

Over time, bail bonds have grown into a promising way of doing business.

Still, the risks involved are as high as the rewards earned. You realize this when you compare the business to other options of investment.

When you decide to bail someone out, it is vital that you fully grasp your obligations ere to submitting your funds for the accused to be released from jail.

Usually, bail bondsmen charge a moderately high fee that could be about 10 percent of the bail amount.

The 10% is the sum that the accused individual will be required to pay once he or she comes back to court.

This is, obviously, a considerable amount to raise in just a few months.

This kind of investment could pose a risk to the investor. In that, the accused individual may fail to turn up for the court process, placing you as the investor in a position that is between a rock and a hard place. In case this occurs, you have a few options.

You could search for the accused person and bring him or her before the court, or pay the full amount of bail bond.

The prior option of tracking down the accused individual on the loose could prove to be quite expensive.

This is, mostly, if you need to work with a bounty hunter whom you need to pay.

Investing in the bail bonds business has only

proved to be sensible if you are familiar with the accused individual and have the confidence that he or she will go back to court when required.

You can never be sure that you will receive your money back.

For this reason, this business needs you to be ready for any possible result following your investment into the bail bond business.

Please note that there are some states that do not permit private bail for profit.

For this reason, bail bondsmen in those states are banned from operating.

Such states include:

- Kentucky
- Massachusetts
- Nebraska
- Maine
- Illinois
- Washington, D.C
- Wisconsin
- Oregon

In these states, other options are used instead of bail bonds.

In case there are no funding alternatives available to the defendant, he or she may be forced to spend their time in jail, waiting for the next hearing.

This may not be a big deal to those guilty of a felony, but it can be a very traumatic experience worth evading for people who are innocent of the crime they are being accused of.

What is a Bail Bond?

To have a clear understanding of a business, it is vital that you understand the product first. In this case, bail bonds are your products.

You have probably heard this statement many times on the news, "The accused has been released on $50,000 bail."

What exactly does this mean? What is bail? How is it different from a bail bond?

When an individual is detained for a felony, he or she is confined in jail until the date of their court case. The judge may decide to release the person on their personal recognizance, or until they are let go on bail.

Bail is, therefore, an established sum of cash that serves as insurance between the defendant (the person in jail) and the court. Paying bail in cash is usually an option that defendants typically have, but as we have seen, many cannot afford it.

Most of the defendants are usually unable to post bail financially on their own. This is because the bail is generally set at a high amount. They, therefore, solicit help from a person who posts a bail bond for them, a.k.a. a bail bondsman or bail bond agent

Therefore, a bail bond is a sort of surety granted by a bail bond company through a bail bond agent. This bond acquires the freedom of the offender from jail.

History of Bail Bonds

When it comes to the American legal system, bail bonds have a long history. They have been in existence in the English legal system since the thirteenth century. Since the American legal system originally stemmed from the English legal system, bail bonds were also borrowed from there.

The start of bail bonds turned into a legal establishment in 1275, as soon as the English Parliament approved the Statute of Westminster. Before this, the sheriffs in localities would either accept bribes to keep individuals from going to jail when they were accused of crimes or lock them up. The ruling clearly stated the crimes that persons would be permitted to post bail for and which they would not be permitted to post bail. This basic system is still the same one used in the United States to date.

As is the case in most countries with liberal economics, venturesome individuals came up with a form of business that entails rendering the services to those that need it. The bail bonds business is pretty much the same. Companies in the industry have been in existence for centuries.

Normally, a bail bondsman will pay up a specific percentage of the bail set on an accused person's bail and place the remaining amount to the court to ensure the defendant is granted his or her freedom.

Though minimal or no changes took place in the bail bonds business over the centuries, the American legal system has done a few alterations in recent years.

The bail bonds businesses that kick-started the industry begun in England soon after the Statute of Westminster. Just like the bail bonds businesses today, their operations were pretty much the same. The individual accused of breaking the law or their family may pay a portion of the bill, and the bail bond business posts the remaining fraction of the bail. This makes it possible for the accused to be free from jail until their hearing.

The United States was part of England and used the English legal system before the Declaration of Independence. When the U.S gained its independence and became a free country, the legal system remained the same with a number of minor developments.

The Bail Reform Act of 1966 was the first key bill pertaining to bail bonds in the United States. This act is a portion of a legislative bill that declares that an individual standing trial for any felony besides murder may be set free on recognizance. This means that there is no need for a monetary bond to be posted.

People charged with very trivial wrongdoing and people with no criminal record are the only ones who can be released on recognizance. It is, however, mandatory for the higher majority of persons indicted of crimes to pay a financial bond.

Shortly after the Bail Reform Act of 1966, the Criminal Procedure Act of 1970 and the District of Columbia Court Reform, approved a bill that looked into the potential risk of the perpetrator to the community. This was done in the District of Columbia.

The reform affected even the individuals accused of capital felonies. Since people who would get out on bail for non-capital crimes would commit crimes at a disturbing rate, the reform was regarded as an answer to some flaws in the Bail Reform Act of 1966.

After the District of Columbia approved this law, there was a significant decrease in the number of people out on recognizance in all jurisdictions. The most updated piece of bill is the Bail Reform Act of 1984, which has had a noteworthy influence on bail bonds in contemporary America.

This Bail Reform Act makes it possible for an individual to be detained devoid of bail if they are a flight risk or are a threat to the public. In most cases, individuals accused of very grim crimes are usually the only ones apprehended without bail.

Market Statistics

Since there are no corporations that hold the lion's share in the market, the bail bond service industry is an uneven industry.

Research by IBISWorld shows that the industry makes an annual income of $2 billion. The report states that from 2011 to 2016, there has been a significant growth of 2.7 percent in the industry. Over the years, there have been more and more bail bond businesses coming up, totaling to more than 24,000 businesses in the United States of America. This has had a positive impact on society as more than 29,000 people have been employed by these companies.

Many people have predicted that the imminent income of the trade shall be highly linked to how the structure of the industry by that time. For instance, a decrease in personal savings is one of the influences that has led to an increase in revenue in the industry. Similarly, a drop in the rate of crimes is expected to have an impact on the growth of the industry.

The bail bonds service industry has had an unwavering development for five years (2011 – 2016). However, the business can be very unsteady, sometimes leading to operators in the industry experiencing a few losses.

Since the law allows bail bondsmen to make use of whatever means to get perpetrators who forfeit their court hearings or bail, this has caused bail bondsmen to work with bounty hunters to make certain that people defaulting on bail are tracked down and presented in court. Some other individuals have their own doubts about the trade and regard it as one that string-pulls the high-risk criminals and the affluent people in society.

With no firm looked upon as major enough to have the leading share in the market or have dominance, the industry has a low level of concentration, making it basically uneven. This has led to the industry having a high number of small and autonomous companies in the industry.

The hurdle for admission for fresh players is very modest. The operators are required to acquire a compulsory license before they can begin operations, as well as act in accordance with the governing requirements as stipulated in the state where they operate.

The past two decades have seen bail bond services making good revenue. This is because 80 percent of the 750,000 Americans that have been to prison could not come up with the money for bail and have no hope of doing so. Only a small number of them will have the ability to meet the bail set through a bail bond service.

This has affected the industry as it has come under a lot of public scrutiny from criminal justice advocacy groups, public officials, as well as media organizations. The players in the industry have been accused of providing services to the wealthy, only leaving those whose bail conditions were set but cannot meet them behind bars to await their trial. In 2009, only thirty-eight percent of offenders were freed since they could meet the bail conditions. About thirty percent secured a bail bond.

Challenges in the Industry

There have been a few challenges in the bail bond service industry over the years, especially from 2007-2011. With the improvement in the economy, the industry began experiencing a rough patch like never before.

Some players in the industry experienced annual losses because more people started saving their money. The savings that people would have would be the one that they would use to pay their own bail.

2008 saw personal savings for customers rising to over 125 percent. This allowed the returns in the industry to drop by over 22 percent. The decrease in the number of felonies committed also led to fewer individuals looking for the aid of a bail bond business, also causing the revenue in the industry to decline.

All was not lost for the players in the industry as

the fortune in the industry improved in 2011. The private savings made by customers began to decrease, thus increasing the demand for bail bonds. This brought about an increase of 1.4 percent, which produced $698 million-plus for that year only. The market share concentration in the industry has generally been low with very few shareholders having substantial shares of the revenue of the industry.

Concentration increased in the industry from 2007 to 2012 because of falling rates of crime being committed, decreasing the number of bails that were to be paid. High overhead costs also made a major contribution to the decrease of players in the industry. In addition, directives by specific states where operators in the industry are being banned from trading bonds are liable for more businesses walking out of the industry. Moreover, a number of states have abolished the payment plan alternative, making it possible for customers to make a down payment on the bail bond and then make payments on a monthly basis. This has had a very significant impact on the bail bond business.

However, all is not lost. There are still many opportunities for anyone willing to get into the bail bond industry, as we shall see later on in the book.

How Do Bail Bonds Work?

Normally, a judge sets a certain amount for bail. In case the perpetrator cannot meet the amount of bail on their own, they are allowed to look for help from a bail bondsman who will, in turn, pay a bail bond.

In order for a bail bond to be posted, the accused is generally obligated to pay the bail bondsman about 10% of the total amount for bail.

The rest of the bail amount is then secured by the bail bondsman as a form of collateral. In case the perpetrator cannot raise enough collateral, the bail bondsman may look for friends and relatives to help in covering the bail.

Often, extra cash payment and the full collateral is needed for a bail bond to be posted.

The defendant's appearance in court after being released is the main determinant of what happens next after the bail bond.

In case the defendant fails to appear in court, the bail bond is forfeited, requiring the court to demand payment of the remaining 90% of the bail.

The defendant's collateral taken by the bondsman will be used to reimburse the court the outstanding bail amount. The collateral may be in the form of stocks, a house, or even jewelry.

If the defendant appears before the court, the bail bond is dissolved upon the end of the court case and the collateral returned to the individual who posted it. In this case, the bail bondsman retains the 10% cash fee as income.

After providing the needed bail for a suspect, the bail bonds business then makes sure that the perpetrator turns up for the hearing in court. In exchange, they acquire the percentage that may range between 8 and 10 percent. Most of the players in the industry are seeking out ways to stand out in the industry, as it is full of so many operators.

The industry has several niches that an operator can deal with, though not many. Several small scale business owners have a preference for offering only one service due to a strict budget.

However, the companies that are running on a large scale can manage to offer all the services pertaining to the bail bonds business.

Some of the niche areas that a bail bond business may choose to focus on are; Deposit Bond, Surety Bond, and Collateral Bond.

For instance, Mike is arrested, and the court set his bail at $15,000. Mike wishes to be free from jail but he cannot raise the $15,000 in cash at the moment. He, therefore, seeks help from a bail bondsman who later posts a bail bond for him.

To post a bail bond for Mike and ensure he is released from prison, the bondsman needs $1,500.

For the remaining $13,500 of bail money, the bondsman obtains collateral from Mike and/or his family. This could be in any form from jewelry, a house, a car, etc.

If Mike shows up at all compulsory court dates, the bail bondsman will need no extra money, thus dissolving the bail bond at the close of Mike's case.

Mike would, in turn, get back his $13,500 worth collateral back. However, the bondsman would keep the $1,000 as a profit that Mike would not get back.

If Mike fails to turn up in court, the bondsman would be required to reimburse the court the outstanding $13,500 of bail. For this amount, the bondsman would have to use Mike's collateral.

If Mike had paid the $15,000 bail amount in cash, he would be eligible for reimbursement at the end of the case, notwithstanding the aftermath of the case.

How Do Bail Bondsmen Make Money?

When someone wants to be free from prison while awaiting trial, bail bonds are the way to go.

The bail bondsman trades the bonds to people who want to be free while waiting to stand trial. They earn a commission from the sale of that bond.

Bail bonds typically cost the same price in most states, which is a 10% charge on the total bail.

This is so for all the bail bond companies, including big corporations. Some more recognized bail bondsmen who have their own businesses sometimes charge a salary that is a bit higher. However, new bail bond agents who have just acquired their licenses can assume a lesser salary rate in order to become established in the industry.

In the bail bonds business, you can grow the number of people you offer your services to. However, this depends on the connections that you make in the field during your entire practice in the industry.

When you own your own bail bonds business, you have a greater potential of increasing these contacts and the number of people whom you serve, simply because you are your own boss.

The income you earn depends mostly on your expertise and experience in your area of dealings. The more experienced and greater your expertise, the more you stand to earn.

If you are just beginning this experience in the bail bonds business, do not lose hope. With time and more practice, you will have opportunities to increase your income.

Regarding the average figures, this is not a set amount of income. You could make more from your business with time, especially when your business earns a good reputation in the industry and becomes a company whose services every client looks for in the industry.

Ways to Make Money

So, you may wonder, how do bail bondsmen make their money? Well, the following are a few ways.

Agreement on Contract

Contractual agreements are one means of earning a living that bail bondsmen use. These agreements are established between bail bondsmen and various courts around the state and city.

They request to post a bond and agree to be permanently bound by the agreement. In response, the court agrees to bail to the defendant out of jail by signature without fronting the money for the deal. The court understands that bail bondsmen will either reimburse the whole amount of bail to the clerk of the particular court or the defendants will come back to court on the set court date. The court is aware that it will receive payment because the bail bonds office agreed to a bond that cannot be revoked.

Bail bonds businesses are now in high demand by defendants who wish to benefit from this sort of pre-organized agreement. This enables the bail bondsmen to grow their business and make plenty of profits. Though from the outside, this value seems to benefit only a few people.

Tangible Assets

When a defendant fails to show up in court for their set court hearing, bail bondsmen earn quite a substantial profit. The bond is called in by the court if the defendants fail to do show up.

For instance, from the example above, if the ten defendants who were bailed out do not appear for their court dates, the bail bondsman is responsible for $500,000. To make sure that this never happens, bail bondsmen need concrete security to act as collateral, like the title to a pricey car, or they place the defendant's home on a lien. In case the bond is forfeit, the office of the bail bonds takes hold of the assets and trades them to recover the money paid out to the court in the form of a bond.

Nonrefundable Fee

The bail bonds law states that the defendant pays a portion of 10 % of the amount of the bail bond before any transaction is done. The 10% is a fee that cannot be refunded, even if a defendant turns up for the hearing on the scheduled date. You can simply make good money from collecting the 10% from bailing out defendants of low flight risk.

For instance, if a perpetrator is asked to post $50,000 bail, the bail bondsman will try to find a signature release of the person and collect $5,000 as prior payment to continue with the bail. If the bail bonds business manages to bail out about ten of such defendants on a weekly basis, they will have earned $50,000.

Typical Salaries

Currently, bail bondsmen make an average annual salary of $25,000. However, after a number of years in the industry, a bail bondsman's income usually experiences a significant increase.

A typical bail bondsman in America received an annual salary of $55,000, from 2009 to 2014. In

2012, the Bureau of Labor Statistics listings of the Financial Specialists' average salary, a group which also includes bail bondsmen, earn an average of $65,000.

Those at the top 10% of income earners make an annual average of $105,000, whereas the last 10% make about $35,500.

The average amount for bail has increased more to than twice the amount, from 1995 to 2010. This has increased from around $25,000 to $55,000. This increase definitely has a ripple effect on the salary of bail bondsmen, with their salaries increasing as well.

Bail bondsmen running their businesses in major cities in the country earned a slightly higher income than their competitors in the region.

In about ten major cities in the U.S, bail bondsmen earned an annual average salary of $60,000.

Characteristics of Bail Bondsmen

Being the best and the most sought-after bail bondsman is not an overnight affair.

It takes having a vast knowledge of people and many years of practice in the field.

With those, you can grow into a guru in the craft. You also need to be a very diligent and patient person.

Dedication and hard work can be very helpful. However, they are not the only characteristics you need to be successful in the business.

As a bail bondsman, you must possess certain qualities and characteristics.

For anyone looking into starting their career as a bail bondsman, below are a few characteristics to have. These qualities will assist you in rising to the top of the business.

A Good Reputation

A bail bondsman's reputation means a lot in the bail bonds industry.

Everybody needs a person that they are sure they can trust with their assets as collateral.

Nobody would want to lose their assets or have problems with the ownership of their assets in the future.

Ensure that your reputation is good and that you can be trusted with peoples' assets, no matter how tempting they are. The reputation of a bail bondsman should be very easy to interpret from the online reviews that your clients give. For this reason, ensure that you have a clean record.

Patience

In this business, you will be dealing with a lot of people. These individuals will be people hoping to get out of jail and who mostly believe that they were apprehended in jail for no particular reason.

With a few exceptions, most of your clients will probably be angry at the fact that they spent time behind bars.

In this case, it is crucial that you practice a lot of patience. You may desire to turn some clients away because of their excessive hostility, but keep calm.

In this business, referrals through word of mouth are the best for marketing yourself. Keep calm and wear a big smile on your face.

24/7 Availability

Yes. People should be able to reach you ANYTIME. The facts on the process of bail bonds should open your mind to the fact that bonds can be posted any time, any day.

Arrests are made anytime during the day or even at night. It does not matter.

If you want to deal with bail documentations from 9 to 5 pm and only weekdays, you may force your clients to spend more time in jail than they would really want to.

For this reason, be the sort of bail bondsmen that is available to post bail any time they are called upon to do so.

Detail Oriented

Being attentive and having a good eye for detail can be immensely helpful in your career as a bail bondsman. Every client will require you to complete a lot of paperwork. For this reason, it is vital that you avoid any mistakes when doing the documentation.

Any mistake, no matter how small, can cost you your business. Therefore, be careful and be keen on details. For your own benefit, observe accuracy in your work.

Good Listener

A good bail bondsman shows the client that they are concerned about them.

No client wants to be just another process and source of income. Every client desires a bondsman that will listen to their circumstances and offer to help them.

Look at it this way. If your clients do not trust you or don't think that you care about them, then how would they turn to you and make you the only connection between you and jail?

They definitely would not. For this reason, you must ensure that you listen to your clients. When you do, you will see how your reputation will grow in the industry.

Good Interpersonal Skills

A bail bondsman is basically required to help and deal with other people that are in need. If you lack the aptitude to interact well with people, then this profession will be tough for you.

In addition, having the ability to decipher the emotions and expressions of people is also a very valuable characteristic to have. In this business, you get to independently choose the client that you want to work with, as well as read and make a decision on persons who you are sure will not skip bail.

Having the capacity to notice dubious individuals during the initial interview can save you the time and trouble spent tracking down a jumper.

Before kick-starting your new life as a bail bondsman, ensure that you have previously had lots of practice dealing with people.

Financial Backing

It is important that a bail bond business has proper financial backing. You will not always have money to bail people out, forcing you to use other people's money when posting a client's bail.

Apart from the 10 percent that they get from clients, bail bondsmen will sometimes use money from their financial backers.

These financiers then earn a profit on their investment from the fees that your clients pay you.

To ensure that you always post your clients' bail appropriately, you must have ample financial backing.

Good Knowledge of Crimes

To become a bail bondsman, you do not have to be an expert in legal matters.

However, understanding basic crimes, their descriptions, as well as the punishments they attract, is crucial when working with people looking forward to getting out of jail.

Ensure that you are familiar with legal concepts and that you also have the capacity to learn fast when needed.

Having Experience

To a bail bondsman, experience is a must-have. Nobody, including you, would want to be constantly worried about having an arrest warrant for them because of their bail bondsman executing their job incorrectly.

Most clients will look for a bail bondsmen with experience and who have been around for a while.

Nobody would ever wish to be arrested and have bail imposed on them. Life can sometimes place an individual at a hard spot.

When you understand this as a bail bonds businessperson, you will find it easy to provide this service to your clients.

Why Should You Start a Bail Bonds Business?

When it comes to bail bondsmen, a lot of people have a biased opinion about what they do. Most of the peoples' opinion is negative, despite the fact that the bail bonding business can be such a well-paying career alternative for a person with the suitable qualities for the business.

A Needed Service

As a bail bondsman, your services are of so much importance to the defendant who has been arrested but does not want to stay in jail until the time of their court hearing. You post bail for the defendant and help them earn their freedom while awaiting trial.

As a bail bondsman, it shall be your obligation to ensure that the defendant shows up in court when they are supposed to.

When you have a clear understanding of the job and its workings, then you will be able to decide if you want to be in the business or not.

Most criminals usually have a bad reputation in the country. However, a lot of the people who are in real need of these bail bondsman services are usually people who are good upright citizens of this country.

Even good people go through challenging times and make poor decisions that would be tough for them to handle on their own.

So, when you offer your services to these clients, you offer them an opportunity to give them a break from detention until their court hearing.

As a bail bond businessman, you also become the clients' source of comfort and support, especially to those who may not have many people around to support them at the time when they are desperate for help.

With the services you provide, you also grow the likelihood of your clients coming back to court to see charges through to the end. Some of them may also resort to changing their lives, correcting their mistakes, and pursuing an upright approach to life.

Depending on how you provide your services to your clients, you may also get some referrals for your business from word of mouth reference from clients you have served.

A Flexible Schedule

A lot of occupations keep people stuck to a conventional schedule. They only get to enjoy a break is when they go on vacation.

However, for a bail bondsman, they perform their duties only when their services are needed by defendants. Therefore, this may make the bail bondsman work very odd hours.

Bail bondsmen can set their working hours at specific times. But then again, it will be more beneficial if your business services are convenient and available whenever they are needed. When you start your businesses, ensure that you observe flexibility, and have a set time of when your business offices are operational.

If you do not need a full-time income, you can offer your services part-time and still earn a good income from it. In case you desire to add to your income, you can provide your services to defendants for more than the typical forty-hour per week schedule.

When you are your own boss in this business, you can choose to take a break whenever you want. It can be very good to take a vacation at any time or be able to handle family emergencies whenever they come about.

Daily Variety

In this business, you never know what is coming your way, or even the sort of person you are bound to deal with. Every assignment is different with different kinds of clients.

Because of this, you can never be too sure who might get arrested and taken to jail or which family may be in need of your help. In this bail bonds career, every single day and challenge is different from the previous one.

If you are not the sort of person who fancies sitting behind a desk all day or handling the same challenges every single day, this career option is exactly the right one for you.

Your responsibilities may take you to different places.

You will find yourself making constant trips to the courthouse and detention facilities in your locality to offer your services to the defendants in need of them.

Once in a while, you may experience a bail jumper with whom you may need to track down and subdue them for failing to show up in court.

Some clients who do not come to court may pose a challenge to you, the experience will take you to different places and will teach you a number of things about the bail bonds business.

Lucrative Entrepreneurship

A lot of people kick-start their journey in the bail bonds business by working for a well-known and established bail bonds firm.

On the other hand, many of them end up

starting and developing their own businesses that earn them a lucrative income.

Once in the business, bail bonds entrepreneurs are free to do their activities their own way, while adhering to the law.

They also get to decide the kind of clients to work with, the most suitable time for them to work, the sort of bonds to offer their clients, and many other aspects of their services.

In this business, you also enjoy the fulfillment of developing your own business as you wish.

You can choose to have the business as security until the time of your retirement or sell your business and leave the industry whenever you want.

Just as in any other business, the choice is up to you as an entrepreneur to do as you wish with your business.

Job Security

Some businesses in this current market usually fluctuate with the changes in the economy.

This makes it hard for investors to predict their

income and make plans to earn a higher income.

However, unlike those businesses with fluctuating rates of income, a bail bonds service will always be a good source of income.

These services will always be in high demand as people will always get arrested everywhere in the country.

According to predictions made by several key organizations, there is a possibility that rates in crime such as theft may rise with time.

This increase is deemed to happen when the rates of economy drop and people lose their jobs.

As long as crime is happening all over the country, you will never lose your source of income in the bail bond business.

This, therefore, makes it a suitable industry for anyone looking to invest in a business that will have a long lifespan.

Types of Bail

Freeing yourself or someone else from jail can be quite a challenging process.

This process is rarely easy due to the fact that one must go through the several kinds of bail bonds offered to him or her.

This means that friends and family can select one type of bail from a vast array of options when paying for bail.

Each kind of bail available to defendants for selection will depend on aspects like:

- Specific offense charged
- Amount of bail
- Your current financial state

As a bail bond businessperson, you should be familiar with all these kinds of bail.

I am going to show you seven kinds of bail that would be available to your client.

Citation Release

Of all the types of bail, this is the best one a defendant can ever get.

This is because the defendant would never really be taken into custody. This sort of bail is issued when the officer arresting the perpetrator does not take the suspect to the police station.

Alternatively, the police grant a citation that instructs the offender to show up in court on a set date.

This type of bail is commonly issued for minor crimes, like a violation of traffic rules.

To get a citation release, the defendant cannot apply or fight for it. Instead, the officer arresting the defendant is the one to choose whether to issue it or not.

Recognizance Release

This kind of bail follows the citation release on the basis of its ease on the defendant.

No money is required, only an assurance from the defendant or their loved one that they will show up before a judge on the set court hearing date.

They will then be released from custody immediately when you sign the paperwork. While no money is charged for release, a fine is set for anyone who fails to appear in court on the set date.

This type of bail can be issued at the will of the arresting officer. On the other hand, the defendant may be required to fight for it in court.

Keep in mind, however, that the fees paid to a lawyer could be more expensive to the defendant than paying for bail.

Cash Bail

This bail is self-explanatory. Bail, in this case, is paid in cash. Any bail can be paid in cash, as long as the defendant has access to the cash. In most jails, cash bail in any other form is usually denied. However, some correction departments accept credit cards, as well as cashier checks.

It is vital that everyone knows the different methods of payment before posting bail.

While it is possible for all bails to be paid in cash, there are several felonies where bail can ONLY be paid in cash.

Normally, this is issued on severe crimes in which the arrested individual is considered a flight risk, but bail cannot be denied.

In such cases, the charge on bail is set so high that it will be impossible for the defendant to pay for it.

Immigration Bail Bond

This kind of bail affects individuals who are non-residents and non-citizens but live in the United States.

It is very challenging to acquire because of the lack of the defendant's legal citizenship status.

For eligibility purposes, specific criteria must be met. This is where your services may be required as a bail bondsman.

To be involved in this sort of bail bond, you must have experience with immigration bail bonds. Years of experience are needed in this case, since it will not be as easy as dealing with a resident or citizen of the United States.

As a bail bondsman, you will also be better suited to give advice to the defendant as required.

Property Bond

These kinds of bonds are not established in all states.

However, the state of California issues them once in a while.

With this sort of bond, all the rights to a certain property must be used as collateral.

There are several kinds of property that can be offered, but people often use real estate.

To get this kind of bond, you must be very patient as it takes time. While some bonds can be acquired in a couple of hours, a property bond requires more time.

An appraisal must be done to determine the value of the property, followed by a court hearing that is conducted to guarantee that everything is settled.

For this reason, it can

take several weeks to secure a property bond.

Surety Bond

This is where the bail bond business is most involved.

As you know by now, a bail bond is a kind of bail fee paid on behalf of a defendant by a bail bondsman.

The bail bondsman is in the business of paying bonds on behalf of criminal suspects.

Once the bail bond agent pays the bail, he or she acts as a surety assuring the court of the defendant's appearance in court.

As a surety, they also tell the court that in case the defendants fail to show up, he or she will pay the full bond amount.

Bail bondsmen make profits from this by collecting a fee of about 10% to 15% of the bail amount from the defendant to be bailed out.

Therefore, if a defendant's bail is set at $10,000, the defendant or his family and friends can pay a bail bond agent $1,000. The bondsman will then act as a surety on behalf of the defendant.

As with property bonds, the bail bondsman usually demands that the defendant or anyone paying on the defendant's behalf, provide some sort of security or collateral against the bond.

The defendant is also required to sign a contract declaring the terms of the agreement.

As we have seen earlier, assets that the bond agent may ask for may be things like jewels, a car, a title deed to some estate, or some other collateral.

The asset should be valuable, in that the bond agent can trade it to get back the full amount of bond, in case the defendant skips the court hearing.

Federal Bail Bonds

The federal bail bond can be used when a federal crime has been committed.

These bail bonds do not require a bail bondsman, as it is done directly in court.

They are almost similar to property bonds. To obtain this bail bond, a defendant can use either cash or property.

Transfer Bonds

This type of bond is different from the other bonds as it is needed when a defendant is in custody in a different jurisdiction.

This could be in another state or another country.

In such cases, the defendant seeks the help of a bail bond agent in the state or country where the defendant is being held.

The process required for signing the bail is pretty much like the local bond process; however, the defendant may be charged extra for it.

The additional fee is issued to the bail bondsman that pays the bond in the particular state or country where the defendant is being apprehended.

The amount of fees charged depends on several factors like the number of bonds that ought to be posted, the defendant's jurisdiction, as well as the distance that the bondsman will have to travel to post the bond.

Starting the Business

Once you are all set to start your bail bond business, you will need to take these next topics into consideration.

Information First

You will need to start with the basics:

- A business name
- An address
- A phone number
- A registered LLC
- A website
- A laptop and office equipment

Create a business name. Ensure that you have a domain name that will be the website address. This way, you can ask people to visit your website that will have your business name, thus familiarizing them with your business.

Get a local phone line through which people can reach you. You can always forward this line to your mobile phone for times that you are not in the office. Technology has made communication way easier these days. You can also buy a Skype phone number that you can use on your mobile phone.

Choose a good office location. This location does not have to be spacious or very well-designed. However, it ought to be the actual address where clients know that they can find you. This location's address will be very crucial on the online listing of your bail bond business.

When launching your bail bond business, it is necessary that you build a proper corporation with the state, registering a business listing, or LLC. There is information that must be readily available for all the forms. Such details include a telephone number and a business address that you will use to complete any legal forms issued by the state and bail applications.

Some states may not allow you to open a bail bonds business using your home address. Also, for safety purposes, it may not be a good idea since you do not know the kind of people that you are bonding out. Always remember that, as much as you want to help, you are not placing a bond for the nicest people in the world. Those who skip may also be upset when you try to find them. For this reason, it is best to separate your business address from your home address.

These days, lots of people prefer marketing online. If you choose to do so, consider using a real address when you start marketing. There are search engines like Yelp and Google that use specific systems to distinguish a real address from a phony one. It is also good to use your business address and phone number when using traditional marketing like newspaper ads.

Obtain advice from a business lawyer with a clear comprehension of the bail system in your state and the insurance required to operate in your state.

Acquire a laptop or a bail bond computer for your business that you can use to track warrant checks defendants' policies, as well as monitor court dates.

Partner with a Well-known Surety Company

This business is definitely very risky. There is no need to sugar-coat that fact. Because of the risk involved, get an insurance company that provides cover to bail bonds businesses. Find one in the state where you will be providing the bail bonds services.

For security, it is also wise to apply at a surety company that you will work when running your business.

To begin working with a surety company, there are bail application forms issued by the state and the company that you will need to complete. The surety company you decide to apply to may provide you with copies of the forms.

These forms used in bail may include:

- Power of Attorney Form
- Bail Source Inquiry Form
- Hold Harmless Agreement Form
- Credit Authorization Form
- Conditions of Release
- Demand Promissory Note
- Schedule Payment Agreement Form

- Bail Bond Application Form
- Mortgage Short Form

Once the surety company approves the forms, your bail agency gets to have a signed license agreement. Ensure that you comprehend the surety company's requirements for your bail bond business.

It is vital that you fully comprehend every financial obligation, the costs of forfeiting payments, any audits and appointments in court, compulsory aboveboard meetings, as well as regular reports on commission.

Acquire State Licensing

In your state, there could be a bail bond board or bail bond insurance. Ensure that you register in any that is in your state or where you wish to run your bail business.

Complete the necessary examinations and background checks, as well as application forms. Ensure that you understand how bail bond businesses are legally opened in your state. Also, keep yourself up to date on the ongoing training requirements required in your state. Keep in mind that every state has different rules and regulations, as well as bills pertaining to bail bonds.

Jail Lists and Registration

Once your bail bonds business is up and running, register your business with the courts in your state where your bail business will be operating. Register your bail bonds business with the county sheriff department and local police as well. This is where you will be writing bonds. It would be good to establish your presence in the necessary centers of your operation.

You will need clients once the business begins. For this reason, you will need to be on the county's jail list, and the bail bonds list at the local jail. This will make it possible for defendants to contact you from the jail.

Read and comprehend the rules and regulations stipulated by the jail on the workings of the bail bonds, and its process. Every jail has its own methods of posting bail bonds. Master the rules and regulations for each jail, as well as the state court.

Pay Initial Fees

To get a license, every bail bondsman must register in the state where he or she runs the business. Every state has its own rules and regulations pertaining to licensing. Every bail bondsman must meet requirements stated by the regulatory bodies for them to acquire a license.

Besides the requirements set out by every state, the bondsman must pay some licensing fees for them to be given a permit. Initially, it may be quite costly starting the business due to fees for licensing, various application fees, plus all courses you need to take to start the business. However, costs vary depending on the state you are operating in.

Some states may charge an initial cost of a few hundred dollars, but the application fees, miscellaneous costs exam fees, training required for licensing may raise the cost of starting the business. This cost may easily amount to over a thousand dollars.

Keep in mind that these expenses are spent on licensing the business only. They do not, in any way, include extra expenses that a bondsman has to incur with other things.

Some of the activities that may add up to the cost of starting the business include:

- Hiring employees
- Printing business cards
- Leasing office space
- Signage
- Office supplies and furniture
- Utility deposits for the office if not included in the lease
- Initial advertising

In some states like Virginia, bail bondsmen are required to retain a bail bonds license as well as an insurance license. In this case, the insurance license has its own supplementary expenses that the bail bondsman will have to pay for.

It is also necessary that bail bondsmen take some continuing education courses on an annual basis after acquiring their license. This is the case for many other licensed professionals in the country. These courses are so important, as they educate one with updated information on the industry. Also, lots of states call for bondsmen to keep renewing their license every single year. For this, there is always a fee charged for the license.

Fulfill Legal Requirements

When becoming a bail bondsman in any state, there are requirements that you will be required to accomplish. These requirements vary from one state to another. Therefore, expect differences in requirements, depending on where you live or run your business.

In some states, the requirements also differ by county. For instance, in Texas, you will find that state laws say that bail bond boards in counties can only be formed in places with 110,000 or more residents. Also, you will find that the requirements in bail bond board counties (CBBB) are poles apart from those in non-bail bond board counties, aka criminal code counties.

In counties with a county bail bond board (CBBB), the bail bond process is monitored by the board. In those lacking bail bond boards, the judges and county sheriff conduct the monitoring of laws pertaining to bail bonds.

So, when applying for the bail bond license, you must meet the following basic requirements.

Proper Credentials

Being in the bail bondsman profession can be quite challenging as one needs to be equipped with knowledge in criminal law, contract law, as well as finance. Therefore, lots of the licensing boards in different states call for bail bondsmen to meet several requirements for them to get the permit to start the business. Most of these licensing boards are normally agencies in the insurance state departments.

For you to become a bail bondsman in any state, you must meet some basic requirements. To acquire a bail bond permit and write a bail bond, the law states that an individual must be of 18 years and above, be of good character as well as trustworthy.

Anybody looking into becoming a bail bondsman must have experience as a member of staff in a bail agency for at least a year and also pass the pre-licensing examination.

These requirements are general necessities in the criminal code county and CBBB.

- Be a citizen of the U.S.A
- Have a GED or high school diploma
- Live in the state
- Never have been convicted of a felony or a misdemeanor crime of moral turpitude
- Be at least 18 years old

In States whose counties have a Counties Bail Bonds Board (CBBB), you are required to also:

- Finish the experience and education requirements for bail bondsmen in the county.
- Own resources of finance that are adequate enough to make insurance available
- Provide an annual financial statement every year. This statement should show details of the resources make it possible for you to provide bail bonds.

Though the bail bondsman licensing process is distinct in

every state, most of the authorities usually have a general process that follows the following steps:

- Show proof of eligibility
- Finish the training and educational requirements
- Do and pass the licensing exam offered by the state
- Apply for a state license

Experience Required

When applying for a bail bondsman license in a CBBB county, you shall be required to provide documented work experience showing your full-time work in a bail bond business. This statement must show that you have worked for at least one year for thirty hours a week.

The documented work is known as an apprenticeship. It must be done in the supervision of a county bail bondsman that has a license of operation. During this apprenticeship, you must have finished all tasks pertaining to being a bail bondsman.

Education Required

In a CBBB county, it is necessary that you complete eight hours of continuing education

(CE) in the classroom before applying for a bail bondsman license. This must be done two years before applying for the bail bonds license.

The CE must be provided at a recognized county university or college and approved by the state bar. You can find listings of CBBB approved bail bond courses on many sites online. Some professional bondsmen in some counties usually provide sponsorship for these courses.

When you have a degree in criminal justice or an area associated with the practice, it can be very beneficial in making you stand out among the multitude of applicants.

The following degrees may provide you with more assistance in the business:

- Bachelor's degree in Business Administration: Criminal Justice

- Bachelor's degree in Criminal Justice

- Associate degree in Criminal Justice

- Associate degree in Business Administration

Though most states require a high school

diploma only to become a bail bondsman, a lot of the bail bondsmen that are most successful usually attend college for further training.

They do so to be fully equipped for the challenges that they may face in this challenging profession. A lot of bail bondsmen obtain a bachelor's, master's, or associate's degree in business administration, law, economics, or finance.

This sort of education can provide immense help to the bail bondsman when performing the duties involved in bail bonding and also when getting ready to sit for the bail bondsman licensing exam.

In a lot of states, the board that handles the bail bond licensing normally has an established pre-licensing course.

This course specifically equips the candidates for the licensing exam that they must take as well as finish up the licensing process. In most cases, this course is usually the first step in learning how to become a bail bondsman as it provides a proper introduction to the basic laws, principles, and practices in the bail bond sector.

This course is usually a wise investment, though not every state demands for the completion of a pre-licensing course for one to acquire the license. It is very beneficial as it provides the bail bondsman with a well-informed and expert foundation for the career in the bail bonds business.

Several instructors in these courses have had extensive experience and practice in the profession, thus can offer firsthand advice and experience to the new bail bondsman.

Pass Your State's Licensing Exam

Most of the states in the U.S offer a state licensing exam. This exam has about fifty to sixty questions with multiple choice and must be concluded within a duration of one hour. This exam is usually given for a fee that ranges from $40-$100. You can find various accredited test providers in your state.

Before taking the exam, it is of significant importance to have extensive information on the exact requirements needed to take the exam. For instance, you can get disqualified from sitting for the exam if you fail to provide a credit card to pay for the submission of fingerprints, as well as a certificate showing the completion of a pre-licensing course. This may be such a loss to the person applying for a bail bondsman license as he or she will lose the fee spent on paying for the exam.

More often than not, states agree to give the candidate the exam several times in case he or she fails.

When applying for a bail bondsman license, the applicant will have to go through a process that normally entails the completion of a certain procedure. Though the process may be distinct to different states, it is generally like the following:

- Submit the application forms and details to the state licensing board

- Pay the required licensing fee. This can be done in the form of a money order check, or credit card

- Submit the results got from the licensing exam offered by the state

- Hand in documents proving the sponsorship of a surety company

- Submit a certain amount for a bond that is mandated by the state

Once you acquire the bail bondsman license, it may be valid for a period of one to three years, depending on the payments you made.

Keep in mind that during the licensing time, several states demand that a bail bondsman finish a number of hours doing the continuing education to qualify for license renewal.

Though laws pertaining to bail bonds are different in every state, most of the states use a similar approach to the bail bonds policy.

Legal Processes Concerning Bail Bondsmen

Professionals in the bail bonds business also work as a surety in court that the defendants will show up in court for their case.

A lot of bail bonds are financial agreements with some sort of collateral that could be jewels or real estate. In case the defendant does not appear in court on the set court date, the bail company is allowed to acquire the property given as collateral legally.

Almost ninety-five percent of bail bonds clients show up in court without bringing up issues, as this sort of risk is normally compelling enough.

Forfeiture

If a defendant fails to show up in court, it can lead to a liability that may lead to losses. In such a case, the bail bond will be forfeited by the defendant, thus the need for issuance of an arrest warrant to the defendant.

When the bail has been forfeited, it is the duty of the court clerk to make the bail bondsman as well as the state's attorney aware of the forfeiture and issue the arrest warrant of the defendant.

Defense of Forfeiture

Since the court is aware that some defendants may forfeit bail, there are laws put in place to protect a bail bondsman from incurring a loss.

The law also protects the defendant from being incarcerated if he or she shows reasonable cause for failure to show up before a judge on the set court date. These laws can lead the court to either cancel part of the forfeiture or the whole of it, postpone any judgment, or order the defendant to go to jail or pay the remaining portion of the bond.

Authority of Arrest

Since a bail bondsman is responsible for the defendant, he or she has the right to arrest the defendant any time prior to the forfeiture.

When going to the authorities to seek an arrest warrant, the law dictates that a bail bondsman must provide a copy of the bond for the issuance of the warrant.

Once the warrant is acquired, the bail bondsman has the permission to arrest and bring the defendant to a detention center or jail. This may attract a financial reward for bail bondsman from the court for tracking down and bringing in the defendant.

Remission

In the ninety days that a defendant is able to turn up in court, the bail bondsman is allowed to either reimburse the outstanding 90% of the bond or bring the defendant to court.

The remission law was formed to ensure that a bail bondsman covers any expenses that were exhausted by the state while in pursuit of the defendant. While a bail bondsman is allowed to apply for a refund, the law allows the courts to counter the bail bonds businessperson if he or she fails to pay those expenses.

Rates of Premium

Normally, bail bond businesses charge defendants a certain amount of fee for them to implement the bail bond.

While the premium is the most important expense that the defendant spends on a bail bond agent, the law also makes it possible for additional money or assets to be collected to pay fees or other costs or for collateral.

For instance, the law in Mississippi permits bail bond businesses to collect fees from defendants for drug testing or electronic monitoring of a defendant that is approved by the court.

A lot of states that allow the bond practice for commercial purposes have the authority to regulate the rates for premiums.

For instance, in Arizona, the rates of premium are put in place by a surety company and then officiated by the director of insurance. There are detailed dollar amounts or percentages stated in the law for bond premiums in at least sixteen states.

Other state rules and regulations on premium rates are designed to ensure that defendants freed on cash bond reimburse some amount of money to the bail bond business prior to their release, instead of allowing the whole amount to be funded.

For example, in Florida, the law forbids the execution of a bail bond devoid of a premium, whereas, in Indiana, the bail bond business must take the full bail bond premium as stated by the commissioner of insurance in the state. In Maryland, the law gives bail bond businesses permission to have their premiums paid in installments.

Banned Locations

When it comes to marketing, states also have laws regulating the locations where bail bondsmen can reach out to clients in person. This is to monitor the way bail bondsmen pursue their new customers.

You will find that the places where soliciting for clients is commonly prohibited are in jails, police stations, and courts. However, there are exceptions to these laws.

For instance, if a bail bond businessman is summoned to the location to carry out some legitimate task or business with a current customer or called by a new client, he or she is usually allowed to get in touch with the client at the restricted location.

Virginia law states that unless a bail bond agent is there on legitimate business, he or she is forbidden from loitering around a magistrate's office or any jail.

Banned Activities

Some bail bondsmen are well connected and have inappropriate interactions with some professionals, particularly those employed by the government.

For this reason, the states have set laws whose aim is to keep bail bondsmen from gaining an advantage in business over his or her competitors in the industry.

These laws are structurally different in various states. In some states, police officers, court officials, or jailers, are banned from telling the defendants about the services of a particular bail bond business. In others, bail bond agents are prohibited from providing incentives of a financial nature to these professionals as well as making any engagements where a bail bondsman gets information from the professional on the status of a defendant.

Bail bond businesses in sixteen states have been banned from talking about the specialized services of another individual with their defendant. Attorneys are the ones mentioned most often. Additionally, a bail bond agent is banned from acting as an attorney, taking part in their customer's trial in any legal capacity, as well as giving legal advice.

Advertisements Regulations

Some states have enacted rules and regulations to monitor the print advertising of bail bond companies. The statute that is most common is the one preventing bail bond businesses from advertising itself as a surety insurance company.

Other regulations pay attention to the clarity of the advertisement. For instance, conspicuously showing the name of the bail bond business, authorizing certain information on contacts, as well as inhibiting the addition of words believed to deceive prospective clients.

Observing the statutes as directed by the law, as well as having the basic requirements needed, you will maintain a good reputation in the industry. This will help as it will increase the number of clients that will come to your business seeking services.

Blunders to Avoid

A lot of bail bond businesses close their doors in the first year of operations.

This is mostly due to the several perilous mistakes they make, which lead to nearly immediate failure. The bail bond business could close when poor decisions are made, thus leading to failure.

On the contrary, you can dodge lots of common mistakes that limit the growth of a bail bonds business with careful planning and expert knowledge.

Let's look into the full picture of why bail bond companies fail as well as deliberate on methods you can use to evade these common mistakes and pitfalls.

Suffering Many Forfeitures

The sort of business that bondsmen deal in consists of a handover of risk.

Since they do not have money to pay for bail, a lot of clients usually seek the services of a bail bondsman.

For this reason, the bail bonds business assumes the risk ensuring that the bail is paid with the bail fee expected in return.

Sometimes, the people seeking the services of a bail bondsman skip bail, leading to the bondsman suffering a huge loss.

In the worst-case scenario, the losses from bail skippers may sum up to millions of dollars, which may cause the bail bondsman to lose his whole business.

For this reason, a bail bondsman must be at ease with the idea of potential risk and the likelihood of huge losses. You cannot be the sort of person who is afraid of working with clients who are likely to skip bail or the risks that may occur at any time.

As a bail bonds business, the biggest problem you can ever face in your practice is when a defendant decides to jump bail and skip town. If the defendant does not comply with the legalities stated by the court for his release from jail, you can be sure that you will incur a huge loss. Such cases are known as forfeited bail bonds.

Therefore, it is essential that you extensively gauge the possibility of forfeitures as forfeitures are the swiftest ways that a bail bonds business can close.

So, in the unfortunate event that a client jumps bail and forfeit the court hearing, the following are the costs you are likely to incur

- The cost of hunting down the defendant who jumped bail.
- In case the defendant is not located, you will suffer the cost of reimbursing the full amount of bond.
- Forfeitures also lead to a risk of

losing the backing of your surety company.

If a bail bonds business suffers forfeitures too often and keeps reimbursing for the bonds, the cost may add up fast. This may then end in a loss of business returns and, in a worst-case scenario, your entire business.

It is important to have rigorous judgment when it comes to evaluating the character of the defendant and/or their cosigner. You can escape such situations when you safeguard the bails that you write.

Forfeitures are common in the bail bonds business. If too many forfeitures happen in one business, it is then a sure bet that your business will eventually end in failure.

To avoid this, ensure that you carry out proper due diligence before posting a bail bond. Do not let bad decisions ruin your business.

Failure to Recuperate Losses

Losses in a bail bond business can be brought about for several reasons. For example, hunting down defendants who have jumped bail, or getting inadequate collateral to reimburse the whole amount for a forfeited bond.

In the event of a forfeiture, the bail bonds company is responsible for either paying the bail bond or tracking down the defendant. As we have seen before, these costs can amount to a large bill very fast.

For this reason, it is vital that the bail bond business assesses which alternatives are less pricey.

Your time in the business should be spent on being accessible for incoming requests to write fresh bail bonds.

Since individuals are getting arrested every hour of every single day, it is vital that you remain accessible throughout the day, to answer these calls round the clock.

Failures in Marketing

Once you get in the bail bond industry, you should not be surprised that you will be facing local competition.

For improved visibility, it is highly recommended that you seek the services of a leading marketing agency.

We live at a time and age when technology has improved and made things easier for very many people. For this reason, it is good for a bail bonds business to get highly active in marketing digitally.

This is the case in all industries as they must implement a concrete plan for digital marketing so as to spread the word to new prospective customers.

Digital marketing is an absolute requirement for anyone looking forward to bringing in new business. To reach out to local clients, it is recommended that bail bonds businesses have a mix of local marketing strategies, SEO, as well as pay-per-click (PPC) services.

It is also vital to have a strong presence on social media if your business is geared towards local customers.

When you expose and reach out to people on social media, you are fulfilling the basic needs of the social media game.

Social media platforms like Instagram, Facebook, and Twitter are leading sites that you must include in your social media marketing strategy for your business.

We'll discuss more about

marketing in a later chapter.

Failure to Face Challenges

Now that you have got some know-how on various mistakes that bail bond businesses made in the industry, you can get ready to face the challenges as they undoubtedly come from time to time.

Running a successful bail bond business never ends. It is an ongoing job that needs effort and nonstop commitment.

When you are in control of your own destiny as a business, there is nothing that can hinder its ultimate success.

The bails bonds business is a risky business. When someone makes a decision to get into this business, he or she must be ready to practically devote their entire day to working with convicts and accused criminals.

In some instances, the clients that a bail bondsman works with may be impulsive and violent.

You can never tell what they will do. They can easily lash out at bail bond agents and target them for their criminal acts.

There have been bail bond agents who have been victims of criminal acts from clients.

Some bondsmen have been injured by angry defendants who were not happy with the results of their court cases, yet the bail bond agents had nothing to do with the decision made.

For this reason, bail bond business owners are at a risk of facing more intimidations and safety threats than most business people in other industries.

Before getting into the business, bail bond business owners must think through ways that they would handle these threats to their business.

They can take steps like hiring guards or installing a security system. Keep in mind that applying those steps does not totally eliminate the potential threat.

You must always be careful and always be on the look-out for anything that may come your way.

A security guard does not come cheap. They can run upwards of $15-$20 per hour depending on their credentials. Some more budget-friendly security steps may include installing a cashiers window with bulletproof glass, as you would see in a gas station or at a large bank teller window.

You can also be sure that your premises has adequate lighting and is in a location near to other 24 hour businsses that will have people around them all the time, just as your business will.

Growing Your Business

So, you have made up your mind to start your venture into the bail bond industry, and the entrepreneurial side of you is taking over. You feel confident that this business is a good course to take.

You understand the requirements needed to open the business. The state board is already aware of your interest to venture into the industry.

Well, before you open your doors to serve clients, it is necessary to be aware that there are skills and tools that you need for your business to survive for the first three years.

You ought to be aware of this before you even sign an agreement with a surety company or sign a big check to pay for your bonding account.

Most people that get into this business are of the opinion that getting clients for bonds would be an easy task because their potential customers are locked up.

A new bail bondsman may assume that their phones will keep buzzing just because their names and contacts are on the jail bond listing.

Usually, this is not the case. A defendant may really need the services of a bail bonding business; however, that does not mean that you will be the one he turns to for the services.

There are so many fish in the sea of bail bonding that the defendant could fish services from.

Therefore, before you get into this business and sign your first bail bond, consider asking yourself the following questions:

- How will your business stand out from the other reputable bail bond businesses and attract customers?

- Which record-keeping software should you use?
- What will your marketing strategy be?

Before you start your business, please keep in mind that suspects in jail that are looking for bail bonds services are not any different from other kinds of customers in other industries. People will return to companies that they are familiar with.

Persons arrested frequently have a tendency to seek the services of the same bonding company every time they are arrested. Call it being loyal, just like they would be to their favorite auto repair shop or restaurant. When you comprehend how important brand awareness and customer loyalty is, then you have the first key aspect required to make your business last long in the industry.

When you are new to the industry, you must develop a concrete plan for marketing your services.

You must demonstrate to your prospective customers why your services are better than other bail bondsmen in the state.

Stand Out

Deeply contemplate on ways you can offer better services and experiences for your customers.

Do extensive research, find the loopholes, and think through an extra service that can distinguish you from other companies. These extra services could be providing better payment plans, offering fair rates at a certain discount, or even providing exceptional customer care services.

You must give the customer a good reason to think of you and call you when they get arrested and become incarcerated.

After you have thought through what will make your business stand out, move to the next step, which is to spread the word.

As a new bondsman in the industry, you must be ready to make imminent prospective clientele know that you exist and are going to provide them with outstanding services.

Choose Helpful Software

Before the grand launch of their business, all new bondsmen in the industry must decide on a case management software that is suitable for their needs. Lots of new bail bond companies take this step lightly and postpone the purchase and installation of the software. After spending some time in their business, they realize how hard it is to catch up when they fall behind with tracking their data.

Once the first bail bond is written, the criminal process has already begun, and the clock is ticking. At first, you may find it easy to know one or two of your clients, but keep in mind that your business may soon grow and start writing bonds for twenty to thirty clients every week. Think of what will happen to your business then. It is wiser to acquire your software management system before you begin your busy service to your customers.

Most developers in the software industry usually offer their customers some time to test their products, thus making the process of selecting software relatively easy. The least possible requirements needed in a bail bonding software are data fields, which handle all the data pertaining to your applications, payment plan reminders, as well as court date reminders.

In the software market, you will also find several businesses that provide software that is web-based and designed particularly for bail bonding. So, when searching for suitable software, take your time and make a wise decision.

Marketing

This is where marketing comes in. To start your marketing, ensure that your business is on a list of bail bonding service providers that are managed by the system at the criminal court. This is only possible if your jurisdiction has such listings in their court system.

You will also need to hand out business cards to prospective customers that you meet in jail or courts. Position yourself in places where you are likely to meet them. You may also need to pay for placing advertisements in periodicals and in different places like pawn shops, public bars, or even bus stops.

Contemporary marketing also requires a business to have a strong presence on the web as customers in the current market are more likely to use a computer or their smartphones to search for bail bondsmen in a certain state.

Marketing Regulations

Now, different states have different rules and regulations on marketing. For this reason, do your research and find out if there are any restrictions pertaining to marketing in your state.

You would not want to be like the Santa Ana bail bondsman who was arrested in 2010 for mailing lots of flyers to convicts and having an arrangement with local attorneys for referrals. He should have been aware that these activities are illegal in the state of California.

Another example would be the bail bond business owners who were sued by a bail bonds business association for giving out flyers in areas around a local jail. The business association termed this sort of marketing as "guerilla marketing."

It is essential that you have a concrete marketing plan that also follows the rules and regulations in your state.

More than Ads

Sometimes, marketing is thought to be the same as the advertising ways and means that companies apply to attract and bring in more prospective clientele to a business. However, marketing entails a lot more than brochures, online ads, newsletters, promotions, or websites.

The actual goal of marketing is to determine and satisfy the needs of the customer as well as determining the particular markets to trade goods and services to. Marketing is defined as "the process of planning and executing the conception, pricing, promotion, and distribution of ideas, goods, and services to create exchanges that satisfy individual and organizational objectives."

To carry out a successful marketing strategy, you should find your target market and understand what the market wants. Advertising is just one of the steps in a marketing plan.

The digital environment in today's world presents both an opportunity and a challenge to small business owners as it is highly competitive. The opportunity is that marketing for businesses has been made easier than ever before. This is because social media helps get the word out faster, and customers have the ability to see the various distinct nature of each brand. This helps businesses by reducing their cost of marketing, acquiring clients, as well as monitoring the changes in the market. Prospective clients get these various brands and information offered online with just a couple of clicks.

There are many marketing tools in this contemporary market. It only takes a bail bondsman who is willing to learn. Below are some current tried and tested ways, as well as a few spot-on techniques that can help you create new business.

Develop Your Brand

The bail bond industry has a lot of agencies out there competing for the attention of the same clientele. Your services will have to be so distinct that they will remember you specifically. Therefore, it is vital that you determine the things about your business that stand out and make you distinct.

If your clients do not know how to get in touch with you or you do not even interact with them, you will not have substantial payoffs. No matter how big and competitive your brand is, communication is key. A lot of current entrepreneurs use email addresses, website names, and phone numbers that are very challenging for someone to recall.

Do not make finding you a difficult process. It may seem easy, but you may not be of the same opinion when you realize how astounding people can forget stuff. When branding, consider using a local number with a series of numbers that are easy to remember or a phone number specifically branded for your business. When it comes to a website domain name, ensure that your website URL is pertinent to your brand and short enough to remember. In it, include your business name as well as the location of your business.

Use Social Media Well

Most people use social media for showing their photos of their daily lives or even those taken while on vacation. Well, social media was not meant for that only. The current social media platforms such as LinkedIn, Twitter, and Facebook, offer great opportunities for businesses to connect with prospective clients and let your prospective customers and contacts know about your business. With these social media platforms, you can get advertising opportunities that make it possible for you to directly connect with the people that you would like to reach out to.

Do not forget that social media keeps changing every day, making it quite a dynamic tool of marketing. Ensure that you are active and maintain consistency in providing content for your clients and contacts. Provide content frequently and ensure that it is of importance to your audience and target market as well as interesting. Ensure that you also minimize on self-promotion and press releases.

Create a Website

Websites are very beneficial in the contemporary market. Your bail bonds website will always be at your service, no matter what you are occupied with.

When building a website, make sure that it can easily be found by prospective clients and convert them to real clientele. This cannot be possible just by creating a website itself. You must rank high in the results on search pages for you to get visitors often. Your website must also be designed in a way that responds and adapts well to screens of any size. This is because most of the web searches are done on tablets and smartphones.

When a visitor cannot get the info they are searching for on your website, they will leave it for your competitor's site. For this reason, make the navigation through your website uncomplicated and clear. This will assist your visitors in finding what they are looking for on your website. When you make information easily available to your customers, you will also manage to boost your rates of conversion.

Be very cautious about what you put on your website and social media platforms. There is some content that assists in boosting the rank of your website in the search engines. It also motivates clients to pick your business over other brands. Ensure that your business, your services, and your contact information are very clear to your clients.

So, what kind of content would make a bail bondsman get more leads?

Content marketing can simply be defined as providing content that the customer is looking for and providing answers to their queries. Therefore, when doing content marketing, ensure that the information you provide is enticing enough to your customers to make them visit your website.

Have vast knowledge about your audience and target market and use a language that is easy for them to understand. Maintain contact and good rapport with your clients. Forget about industry professionals and lawyers. Maintain a friendly approach and keep your content simple. You can talk about topics such as "What is the difference between bail and bond?" and "What happens when a defendant jumps bail?" Such topics will assist in bringing in more visitors to your website.

To lead in content marketing is not an easy task. Nevertheless, you can use several steps of search engine optimization to take you to the top of the Google search in your locality. As you post more information related to bail bonds on your site, you will notice a rise in the rank of your business online. This will, in turn, have a ripple effect on tour business.

When developing your website, ensure that you select a style that is responsive.

By responsive, I mean that the website should be readable and fit on a screen of any size.

A lot of customers in the current market leave their computers at home for the ease of mobile devices.

As for bail bond businesses, it is highly expected that the prospective clients in the industry usually do the same thing.

Desktop searches are now outdated and outpaced by mobile devices as of 2015. Google recently began to formally give search engine preference to businesses whose websites are designed for mobile use. If your website is not enhanced for mobile use yet, then you will suffer poor placement on the main Google results.

Therefore, take advantage of the opportunity mobile devises provide. Do not create a website that does not work well with mobile phones or tablets, as that will negatively affect your online marketing. If possible, create a mobile app that will make it possible for you to easily and effectively communicate with your clientele.

Do Online Paid Advertising

One of the unquestionable methods of bringing attention to your business is by gaining a boost from paid ads in search engine campaigns. These are the search results that appear on the top of your screen, as well as the side of search results.

Initially, pay-per-click (PPC) advertising is quite effective in online advertising. It has helped many businesses get their names on the front line for potential clients. However, the dynamics of the current market have had an effect on the methods of advertising.

As a bail bondsman, you should put your focus highly on cost-per-click (CCP) advertising, which has very effective results. Google ads and ads on Facebook make it possible for one to select a particular pay-per-click audience that will see your advertisements occasionally. Therefore, ensure that you reply to messages on social media quickly. Remember you are paying for every click to your website.

Another great way you can connect with your customers through Google search is to take advantage of the organic and unpaid search results. Imagine how strong your marketing would be if you combine the power of both?

Do extensive research and develop a strategy that will make sure that you appear on the first page of search results over time. Use search terms that have a high probability of being used by customers. Do not worry about the money that you use to pay for advertising. That investment will pay you more than you spent in a reasonably short period of time.

When you combine both tried and tested marketing techniques and the current digital techniques, there is no doubt that you will be a killer brand in the bail bonding industry. Use the best of both worlds and see yourself standing out from your competitors and earn more opportunities to provide your products to your clients.

Mentions

When a business is mentioned on social media, apps, or websites where clients are likely to look for your business, that mention is known as a citation. Different factors can be mentioned about a business from their address, business name, phone number, or website. Sometimes a business can also get an entry to Google Maps and have their information appear in a reliable format, thus a structured citation.

You can also have an unstructured listing on an article, blog post, or social media site. The business information may be included within a story or in a paragraph on a social media post.

When you have these sorts of references, web users easily locate businesses in the locality, thus boosting the rankings in the search engine.

With good citations, you can be guaranteed of good business. So, wherever your business appears online, claim it so as to keep your listings up to date and spot on.

The following sites are good for bail bonds business citations:

- expertbail.com
- bailbond.com
- citysearch.com
- yellowbook.com
- yellowpages.com
- manta.com
- local.yahoo.com
- aboutbail.com
- superpages.com

Maintain a Personal Link

Although the world has become highly digital, there is nothing like a face-to-face meeting or introduction. Taking a personal marketing approach may consume much of your energy and time. You will definitely not do this in a few clicks on your smartphone. However, it is worth the effort.

When everybody else is staring down at their phones, you can take a different approach and look up and shake a few hands. Believe me. You will be outstanding in this generation's market.

Besides the current digital marketing, you can also use traditional bail bond business marketing techniques that also add a personal touch to your marketing.

Such traditional advertising may include physical advertisements in the area near a jail or detention center, like, placing signage on vehicles, or signs on buildings. While these methods might seem outdated, these marketing techniques are still very effective for businesses in the bail bonds industry.

Give your advertising a personal touch and see how fast you will bring in new business.

Customer Service Skills

Bail bonds companies are distinct in their own ways. They seem to take two different approaches in the way they interact with their clients.

There are those who choose to see their defendants as clients and not criminals, and those who choose to view their customers as guilty until proven innocent.

I would strongly advise that you see the defendants as clients and not criminals. Companies that take this approach are excellent in the way they provide their customer care service to their clients.

For the most part, they have these five qualities in common.

Expertise in Bonding

It is essential that every bail bondsman has detailed knowledge and be an expert in their profession.

Yes, as a bail bondsman, you need to be well acquainted with the general workings of the system. You must also be familiar with the requirements, rules, and regulations in your state. Without information on your practice, you will barely be able to provide proper services to your client.

It would also be very helpful to have established connections with persons in the justice system.

You will need people you can get in touch with for advice or for services like tracking down a defendant that has jumped bail or to get your defendant a quick release.

Ability to Patiently Explain Things to Clients

Besides having vast knowledge in your area of expertise, you should also be very good at explaining things to your client. Since most defendants or their loved ones are not familiar with how bail bonding works, you need to patiently explain the workings to them as well as their loved ones. With that, you will help them get exposure and comprehend the bail bond system. You and your employees must be patient, understanding, and be able to make information available for the client.

Empathetic

Most defendants in need of a bond are usually very emotional, and in a not-so-peaceful state of mind. You should understand this as a bail bondsman. Be empathetic and approach the situation as if you were in their shoes and do the necessary things required to be of help to them. Keep your spirit up throughout the entire process and make them feel like you understand them.

Have a Positive Attitude

Without a positive attitude, you are likely to fail as a bail bondsman.

A good bail bondsman will give off a positive vibe when working with his or her different clients. Some clients will not be very easy to deal with, as they are in a stressful situation. However, do not make them bring your spirit down as you work with them. Maintain an attitude showing that you can handle any situation and commit yourself to attaining your defendant's freedom.

Once they are free, your clients then have the ability to make sound decisions with regards to legal strategies and bail bonding agreements. This way, you will be able to better handle them without the stress that they were in previously.

Offer Fast Service

As a bail bondsmen, you should commit yourself to earning your clients their release as early as yesterday.

This means that you should be available and easy to locate, preferably near state centers dealing in law enforcement. You must have all the tips and tricks needed to get your client out of jail as soon as possible.

Do your best to ensure that the defendant does not spend another night in prison without a conviction. When you do so, you will get many new clients from referrals.

Dealing With Bail Bond Jumpers

When bondsmen get into the industry, they sometimes take bond forfeiture lightly.

Most of them assume that defendants will return to court on their own and that forfeiture is the only reason why a defendant must be taken back to jail to rid the business of legal responsibility. But this is not the case.

There are many factors why a defendant must be returned to jail.

These factors include new arrests, the defendant trying to flee from the state to hide, as well as unpaid bond premiums.

When you have these in mind, you will know that it is very important to have a bail enforcement professional on standby for times such as these.

Now, it can be quite a task when hiring bail enforcement professionals that are excellent at their jobs. Finding a really good one may take a long time.

While in search of bail enforcement agents, you will come across some who identify themselves as bounty hunters, fugitive recovery agents, or bail recovery agents. Take your time and choose wisely, as finding one that is suitable for your business can be a bit tricky.

All business owners should be eager to make constant changes of strategies to be able to keep up with the ever-changing market and economy.

Once your business develops, you may experience a change in your target demographic or an increase in the number of bond violations. For this reason, it is vital that you remain flexible.

All About Bounty Hunters

Pick a Skilled Bounty Hunter

Good professional bounty hunters usually

have a lot of bail bondsmen calling them on a daily basis. So, when finding a bounty hunter, you must find one that is well-known and recognized in the state as the best in his work.

Once you find a professional bounty hunter, you will be sure of a non-problematic process in getting back the bail jumper. It is important to look for a bounty hunter with an established track record of his work, one that fulfills all your needs in tracking down the bail bond jumper.

Keenly look into skills, previous work done, or any reviews about certain bail enforcement agents. This is because when you hire a bounty hunter or bail recovery agent that does not fit the needs of your business, you may land yourself in big trouble in the future which may limit your growth or even lead to bankruptcy.

In case of any liability, the bail agent enforcer is fully responsible for fixing the problem. For this reason, the bounty hunter you choose must be really good at their job.

When looking for an excellent bail enforcement agent,

there are several factors that you should consider:

- His character and personal conduct
- How many fugitives has he arrested
- How he relates to perpetrators and their families
- Is he respectful and courteous to the client, or does he treat them with hostility and contempt?

When customers get angry because of a bounty hunter, this could erode the reputation of the company from negative advertising through word-of-mouth, thus leading to the loss of clients.

With a professional bounty enforcement agent that is an expert in the area, you can be sure that your bail bondsman business will last for several years as he will ensure that the liabilities the company faces are well dealt with.

Every time a bail jumper or fugitive is arrested, you will not suffer any obligatory bond payment. You will also have a good reputation in the industry as you will be known for taking any liability that you face seriously.

Involving a Bounty Hunter in the Bail Bonds Business

When someone mentions a bounty hunter, the picture that comes to mind is of a Wild West cowboy on his horse, riding to different places in pursuit of a fugitive.

We imagine the bounty hunter with a poster in his saddlebag with the picture of the wanted fugitive. And of course, the image of a bounty hunter is not complete without a gun well secured around his waist.

Well, that image is not totally false.

Throughout history, the responsibility of a bounty hunter was to bring back the fugitive/bail jumper dead or alive.

In the Wild West days, the bounty hunter's main interest was to collect the fee paid for finding the fugitive. This has not changed much as many bounty hunters are interested in pretty much the same thing.

When a bail bondsman's client skips the bond and moves to another city or state, it can be quite disappointing for the bail bond businessperson. In such a case, the bondsman usually resorts to measures aimed at finding the defendant so as to evade reimbursing the full amount of bond imposed on the defendant by the court.

This situation calls for a bounty hunter who comes to do his duty, which is to locate the bond jumper. However, unlike the bounty hunters in the Wild West, the defendant MUST come back to your jurisdiction alive.

How Bounty Hunters Work

To a bail bondsman, a bounty hunter is more or less an ever-present help for him or her at all times. For you to fully comprehend how the bounty hunting business works, let me explain a bit of how they contribute to the business and exactly how bail bondsmen need them.

So, you write a bond for your client who is charged for a felony and ensure that he or she leaves jail and stays free the whole time before their hearing. After the bail is set, you pay the bond and act as an assurance that the defendant will come to court on the set date of his or her own hearing. So, you do so and charge the defendant the usual 10% of the total amount of bond.

As a bail bondsmen, you work as an insurance company that endorses the bond. You have the authority and power of bail that may sum up to several thousand dollars depending on the number of bonds you sign.

As a bail bondsman, new in the industry, you will be obligated to keep what is known as a "buildup fund" for moments when a defendant skips bail. The purpose of the buildup fund is to pay out the bonds to the courts in case the defendant skips bail. Forfeiting bail is known as an estreature. This buildup fund is reserved from a portion of the bail bondsman's commission from the writing of the bonds. The assurance company will only release a limited amount of bail powers to the bondsman until the bondsman buildup fund totals to a certain amount, and his track record of writing good bonds is confirmed.

If a defendant skips town and does not turn up for their court hearing on the set date, you may have to incur the whole cost of bail sooner or later. The period of time you have to incur the cost varies from one state to another. It could range from a month to a couple of years, depending on how your state operates.

In case you fail to bring the bail jumper back to jail or court, you shall suffer quite a substantial financial loss. You will lose your good reputation before the eyes of the assurance company, as well as the court. It is, therefore, of much advantage to you that you track down the bail jumper, have them arrested, and bring them back to court for their hearing.

Most bondsmen remain hopeful that after issuing an arrest warrant, the defendant will be found and arrested by the police. This may take time and make the bail bondsmen anxious as the grace period for bringing the defendant back to court draws nearer by the day. In such a case, the bail bondsman begins to lose hope in the police and seeks the help of a bounty hunter who is an expert in the area of tracking down fugitives.

When a bail bondsman looks for a bounty hunter, he has reached a dead end and has no other option. The defendant has skipped and cannot be found. Also, the bail bondsman may look for a bounty hunter to skip a finder's fee that is more expensive than a bounty hunter. In addition, it is important that he maintains a good relationship with the assurance company and is doing all he can to avoid future losses.

Bounty Hunter Fees

You may be wondering how much it would cost to hire a bounty hunter. Well, I would say that they are much more affordable than the amount of money you stand to lose if you don't.

A bounty hunter's finder fees usually vary depending on how complicated the case is and the bond amount. A high amount of bond will attract a high bounty hunter fee, whereas a smaller bond will attract a finder fee that is much lower.

The most recognized hunters are mostly the ones that are in a position to ask for a retainer fee from the bondsman. A lot of cases are dealt with on strict contingency, meaning that a large portion of the bounty is not paid until the fugitive is apprehended.

Some bounty hunters have established themselves in the industry by providing their tracking services for free.

They do so as a way to market themselves and show their skills to bail bondsmen. For this reason, do not be surprised when a bounty hunter comes to your office to offer his services at no charge. This way, you can get to establish a trustworthy relationship with the bounty hunter after he has shown his expertise in their tracking duties.

After that, you will be able to seek his services any time you have a bail jumper and you know that the bounty hunter is capable of providing services with good results.

A Word of Caution

More often than not, bounty hunters are in great demand in the bail bonds business. Any bail bondsman will do anything to get a good one. However, one must be careful.

The industry is full of deceptive people who are good at marketing themselves as bounty hunters, yet have no clue what the business entails. This business is a good hub for dodgy characters who are more criminals than professionals. With such people around, the reputation of the bail bond industry gets diminished and brings about a misunderstanding with the law enforcement system.

As you look for a bounty hunter, keep in mind that the market only has a few professionals who can provide excellent services to a bail bondsman.

Dealing with a bail bond jumper is one of the hardest tasks you would ever come across in the business. Therefore, ensure that you get the right person with the expertise required to handle the job to success.

How Bounty Hunters Operate

The bail bondsman will certainly provide the bounty hunter with a copy of the bail agreement before any attempt to pursue the defendant. He will also give the bounty hunter a power of attorney to do his work as an agent of the bondsman.

A professional bounty hunter also retains with them a copy of the 1872 decision of the U.S. Supreme Court. It is also vital that a bail bondsman has a written agreement stating the fee of the bounty hunter before he starts tracking down the defendant who has skipped bail.

In county courthouses are civil records that bounty hunters usually use to find cases of a bond skip. There are many such cases that are usually filed by insurance companies and bail bondsmen with bail skippers that the hunter can track down.

In some instances, bounty hunters find the skippers to several such cases in less than half an hour. Sometimes a bounty hunter may set out to find the bail jumper before even obtaining the assignment from the bail bondsman.

This may take hours to a few days.

Once the bounty hunter finds the bail jumper, he contacts the bail bondsman involved in the case and strikes a deal on the finder's fee.

As a bounty hunter, you can make a deal before making an attempt to arrest the bond skipper.

Normally, a bail bondsman usually has a bounty hunter in their contacts that he or she can call any time. These contacts are obtained from sales calls that are often made to bail bond business offices.

Insurance companies also seek the services of an established bounty hunter at various times in their operations.

Sometimes bail bondsmen move to other states and hide after a defendant skips bail because he or she is not able to incur the whole cost of bail. There are many people who make attempts to make a living in the bail bonds industry but fail terribly, running out of money in the first few years.

In such cases, the assurance company will seek the services of a bounty hunter to track down the bail bondsman. Posters with wanted persons are usually issued by insurance company offices just like the old times in the Wild West. This way, bounty hunters usually register themselves on the mailing listing at insurance companies so that they can get copies of those posters of wanted persons first hand.

Not Just Anyone Can Be a Bounty Hunter

It is vital to note that the bounty hunting business is not meant for just anyone, as it is quite a challenging occupation. The bounty hunter takes dangerous steps to hunt down fugitives and their ultimate job is to track down and arrest hardcore felons.

Sometimes, the bounty hunter may be required to use force when pursuing a defendant and bringing them to custody.

There are also very complicated methods put in place when carrying out the actual tracking process. These tracking techniques can be very hard to enact.

In their career, bounty hunters often come across some hardcore criminals who are involved in different felonies such as human trafficking and prostitution, selling drugs, or dealing in stolen merchandise.

Tracking such people very often involves experiencing some felonious side of the law, yet most bounty hunters follow the set government rules and regulations.

The business is meant for those daring enough, and with the required skills, to set out and find such people and acquire a huge finder's fee.

So, as a bail bondsman, it is good to have a

bounty hunter in your contact list. This way, you will be able to get good tracking services that will save you a huge amount of loss that you would incur if you do not find the bail jumper.

Thinking Like a Bail Jumper

So, you have got a client, paid their bail, secured some collateral – the whole bonding process – then your client decides to skip town and hide in another state. Though there is a high likelihood of such an occurrence in the bail bond industry, it will definitely not be a good experience since your business may suffer loss.

However, all is not lost. There are several ways to deal with a bail jumper.

But first, let us look into the psychology of a fugitive, running away from their responsibility or justice.

How exactly do they feel? What is usually on their minds?

Well, the experience is usually fairly uneventful for most bail jumpers. For example, when one jumps bail and skips town prior to their set court hearing, he or she may be declared a fugitive.

In most cases, they will not be exposed to a manhunt all over the nation, except if they were arrested and charged for grave felonies. Normally, the police in other states will not follow you or do a high adrenaline car chase through the city.

It doesn't happen like you see in the movies!

It seems like a safe thing to do, right? Well, the answer is no. Jumping bail will not be easy for the defendant to do. Since skipping bail has grave consequences for the bail bondsman as well as the defendant, the bail jumper will constantly remember their situation and try their best to keep a low profile. They also know the consequences that they will face in the case they are arrested and taken back to court.

Before going any further, let me first explain the consequences that a bail bond jumper is likely to suffer when they get arrested again.

These consequences must be explained clearly to the defendant before writing any bonds.

Consequences of Jumping Bail

You can hunt down and rearrest the defendant who jumps on his bond in any state and any city in the United States. The defendants usually sign away a few of their rights when they are bailed out on bond by a bail bondsman.

The law also makes it clear that the rearrest can be performed by another agent who is appointed by the bail bondsman.

The bail bondsman or bounty hunter operations have been established and given authority in the United States. The *Taylor vs. Taintor* Supreme Court decision is where the bounty hunter operates and is the highest authority from 1872.

The case states:

"Whenever the bondsman or bounty hunter decide to do so, they may get hold of the fugitive and deliver him back in court. They have the permission to hunt him down to another state as well as arrest him on the Sabbath. The law also allows them to break in and enter his house for the purpose of finding the defendant. No process is needed for finding a bond jumper. Many compare to the arrest of an escaping prisoner by the sheriff of a county."

This law has often been misunderstood, even

though the rights of a bail bonds business and its agents have been in existence for ages. Even most law enforcers are not privy to the real law.

In 1984, Dave Mollison's Freedom bail bond business got two of their bounty hunters detained in Ohio on charges of kidnapping in an attempt to pick-up.

Tim Johnson brought Jaffie, a defendant who had skipped bail and ran away to Canada back to the state of Florida. This brewed an international mix-up causing an episode of strain with the government of Canada and the United States State department in 1982. Johnson was charged for kidnapping.

Bail bondsmen have several options of dealing with a defendant that jumps or skips bail by failing to show up for their court hearing.

Instead of incurring the whole cost of bail because your client has left the city or state, you can use any of the following ways to bring them in.

Apply for a warrant of arrest for the defendant.

If a warrant of arrest is issued, the police in the

region will be informed that the defendant jumped bail. This way, everyone can be on the lookout for them. With an arrest warrant, the defendant may be pulled over on their way to another state because of a usual traffic violation and get arrested.

You may have the driver's license of your client suspended.

In such a case, the defendant will not be able to use his or her driver's license until the suspension is lifted.

You can sue your client for jumping bail.

Depending on the state you operate in, you could sue your client for contempt of court or failure to appear in court. This could attract an extra jail term or fine for the defendant, in the case that they are found guilty.

You could sue and have the court raise the amount they will have to pay for his or her bond, even if bail was already posted.

If the defendant did not have to pay the bail bond and was released on recognizance, then he or she will most likely be required to pay the bond once they are back in prison.

Ask the co-signer.

Since most defendants usually have a family member or friend as a co-signer, you could approach them and have them reveal the defendant's location or face the consequence of paying for the full bail bond themselves.

If a friend or family member posted your bail for you, you've left him or her in a bad situation. If not, they will have to surrender the assets used as collateral.

Conclusion

So, as you already see, the bail bonds business is a potentially lucrative business. With the right character and attitude, you can make a good income for yourself and also provide employment to others for a long period of time.

People will be break laws and be arrested at any hour of any day. Crime rates are not dropping, and people's savings are usually not enough to cover bail. Your career as a bail bondsman can be assured.

While the business is risky, it can give you an income that will sustain you for years. If your dealings in the business are legal, adhering to the rules and regulations as stated in the law, then you can be guaranteed of growth in your business and a long lifespan.

Do not ignore the risks. Think them through and take the necessary measures that may reduce them. Build up relationships with people involved in the industry like lawyers, bounty hunters, law enforcement agents, amongst others. These people will help you get through with your duties faster and more effectively than when you work alone.

Get in the business and experience the sweetness of being of help to defendants who need this vital service.

If this book has informed or inspired you, please consider leaving a review wherever you purchased this book. I will read all of the comments and take them to hear to improve my future writing endeavors.

www.ingramcontent.com/pod-product-compliance
Lightning Source LLC
Chambersburg PA
CBHW070645220526
45466CB00001B/301